Whose
sofa
is it
anyway?

NICOLE RÖDER

Whose sofa is it anyway?

A light-hearted look at training
pitfalls and how to avoid them

CADMOS

contents

Copyright © 2008 by Cadmos Verlag GmbH, Brunsbek
Copyright of this edition © 2009 by Cadmos Books, Great Britain
Cover design and layout: Ravenstein + Partner, Verden, Germany
Cover photo: Anneke Krems
Photos: animals-digitals, unless otherwise indicated
Illustrations: Frank Fritschy
Editorial (English edition): Christopher Long
Translator: Alexandra Cox

Printed by: Westermann Druck, Zwickau

British Library Cataloguing in Publication Data
A catalogue record of this book is available from the British Library.
Printed in Germany
ISBN 978-3-86127-962-4
www.cadmos.co.uk

preface

How not to train your dog

Every single day, we dog-owners use up a whole load of energy mis-training our dogs. As a result of the many apparently trivial communication and handling difficulties that keep cropping up, with the best will in the world we appear to focus all our efforts on turning them into companions that are never going to fit in with our everyday lives, the dogs that we never wanted to have. Everybody else seems to pull it off, but we just can't. Yet it could all be so easy.

Even in times when, in some parts of the country, a person can only venture out of doors with a four-legged friend under cover of the night (after all, one is providing a home to a dangerous beast and parading it in public, to boot), one mustn't assume the blackest point of view. Life with dogs is (mostly) a wonderful experience that is a lot of fun and gives us a whole lot to laugh about – even if we do occasionally wish the ground would swallow us up when our well-bred quadruped just cannot keep himself to himself at the restaurant again and tries to drive away an intrusive fellow canine in an eardrum-bursting frenzy of barking. How is he meant to know that the other diners aren't bothered by this alien's intrusion and that his beloved human isn't at all willing to back him up, but is only hunting about for the 'off' button?

I am not very fond of these moments, when strangers turn round to look at me and my 'damn dog' and start whispering because, yet again, my years of training efforts have failed to come to fruition. Yet I love milking these funny-because-embarrassing stories when meeting my friends a few days later, as I pat my dogs' heads and tell them: 'You really are the biggest darlings a person could wish for.' There is no coin without the other side, no cohabitation without pain and no dog-owning without tears and laughter.

In this book I am going to take a look at typical upbringing errors and comment on them from our dogs' point of view. Not entirely seriously, but with a good pinch of irony and a permanent wink of the eye – true to the motto: It will all be fine (in the end)!

Have fun with this book and even more fun with your four-legged friend!

Oh, these impossible bipeds!

A pampered little infant pooch like this one is a real bundle of surprises and sometimes grows up faster than we think.

How we gaze lovingly at this little puppy that lies slumbering in his basket and, apart from eating and playing, doesn't have many interests yet! A harmless canine infant with the world at his feet, as innocent as innocent can be. A cute little angel that we have brought home, just waiting to become the perfect companion in our everyday life.

Yet, barely six months later, this little angel may have grown into a little devil with few apparent remaining traces of innocence when he sinks his sharp teeth into our trouser-legs; when he shoos a flock of birds right across a field and simply ignores our enraged yells; when he suddenly begins to bark at everything and everybody that appears to be his rival and we are left standing there, helpless. When this happens, once again we look around for that hole, longed for and yet never appearing, that we can crawl into.

How did it come to this? How could that tiny, cuddly, innocent lamb have turned into a dog that goes berserk in certain situations? There must be something in the genes! Or maybe not... Could it be that it may have just a tiny bit to do with our upbringing methods and communication between human and dog? Don't we humans sometimes behave a bit idiotically when it comes to training? In this chapter, we're going to take a closer look at misunderstandings during dog training – and one of the ways we're going to do this is from the point of view of our beloved four-legged friends. Things might seem a little bit clearer for us then.

Right at the very beginning I would like to mention a classic example where the behaviour of bipeds doing the upbringing – which is a bit puzzling from a dog's point of view at times – is elucidated in closer detail:

Tests of patience

With all the groups of young dogs that I have led so far, almost all participants had the problem that their dogs refused to come when called on walks. A young dog is discovering the world and still testing how far his biped's patience and, above all, consistency will stretch. Dog-owners often tend to fire off their orders in volleys of four or five charges in rapid succession.

What does the dog learn?

No

Obeying after the first command is totally unnecessary, as experience shows that I'll be asked to follow orders at least twice more.

Oh, these impossible bipeds!

'Time to go on the lead again? That's a real shame. I was just really beginning to suss out the situation.'

Because many people tend to yell out their orders several times, one after the other and almost without a break, the quadruped very quickly learns that there's no need to rush. Hearing, 'Come on, Sammy! Here! Come on! Come here, now!' in the woods is virtually the norm for him by now. Yet, astonishingly, you very rarely encounter dogs that start making their way to their owner right from the first 'Come on'.

Whether it's sit, lie down or coming when called that's required, every cue must be given only once. This is the effective way to help our four-legged friend follow the command.

Recall is one of the most important training exercises in a dog's life and, as such, should be practised with appropriate frequency. If the dog fails to come on the first call, either we go and fetch him (even if he is in the process of playing with his pal and we are the last thing on his mind), or we stomp off loudly away from him while he is taking a sniff at something interesting and taking all the time in the world before coming to us.

As soon as he has caught up with us, or as soon as he comes running up

13

behind us, he gets loads of fuss and attention (or, if he's not quite caught up with us yet, attention in the form of ringing verbal praise). Whatever the situation, the idea is to make it fun for the dog to run to his human, because with the human close by, action and fantastic surprises are guaranteed. The way a young dog sees it, getting called is generally a pretty stupid thing – people always seem to want you to come when you're a young dog in the middle of discovering something great and having enormous fun.

With some people, the tone of voice they use becomes more and more aggressive, the more often they call, with the result that an intelligent dog will think twice before running up to them; if they're yelling as angrily as this, it is definitely not clever to run straight up to the human, because whatever's going on, it can't be good when they're using such a funny tone of voice. But the very, very worst thing of all is when you're with your folks and they put you on the lead. All the fun is over and you have to behave and walk nicely alongside them again.

Indeed, it is often the case that people only ever call their dog during a walk when they want to put him on the lead. Why not call out the dog's name every now and then just to reward him,

The dog draws the following conclusion: if you ignore your owner's calls for long enough, the walk will last longer.

throw him a toy or whatnot and then send him off on his way again? If you do this, the dog will learn that it really is worth his while to come on the first call, as after all we could be up to something great that he really doesn't want to miss.

Dogs that wander off out of their biped's sight at the first opportunity generally do not do this because they have seen something interesting. They are looking for the excitement that is not on offer from their humans. Young dogs, especially, want stimulation for their minds and aren't interested in just trotting along the path. Boredom, even on a walk, is poison for the human - dog relationship. This in no way means that we bipeds need to be around-the-clock dog entertainers, but always being more interesting than the surroundings helps stop the dog from being dragged into boredom or left to

'She's bound to call at least twice more, so I've got plenty of time...'

his exploratory musings, which not infrequently come to a halt in front of a car's bumper because of that leaf that's been fluttering back and forth in such an interesting way across the road.

This is only one example of many that shows how we, as dog-owners, unwittingly enable problems to develop. 'My dog does not come when I call him,' is a problem that's recounted to dog trainers a thousand times a day, and in most cases it is the humans who have got their dogs into this habit.

'Fantastic! I'll just howl the place down a bit more. Then we'll be moving again and, if I'm lucky, I'll get a treat as well.'

The way to do it

Make yourself interesting for your dog. Also, give precise consideration to what you expect from him. Practise cues consistently and view situations the way your dog sees them.

Encounters

Here is another common misunderstanding between quadrupeds and bipeds, elucidated from the dog's point of view:

The beanpole has stopped yet again. We've only just got going, and we've only got a few metres to go before I can finally enjoy a bit of freedom without this stupid restrictive thing around my neck. But no: he's exchanging funny noises with the other bipeds, and they're feeling the need to do it right here and now of all places, standing around. Can they not communicate on the move? I want to get away – come on, get going! I'll mention that to him now, maybe he'll understand that I'm bored. (Barks.) Great, he's actually noticed me and talked to me. That's some progress, and he's not as calm now as he was before I barked. Surely that means we can get going now. But he's still showing no sign of moving. I probably need to push him a little more and tell him again, and while I'm at it, I'll be a bit louder and shout for longer, that'll get him listening to me, because this is just so boring. On my own all day, and now we're getting no further, even though there's absolutely nothing, nothing whatsoever, to do here. Nothing to sniff at, nothing to learn – it's grim, and he's standing there. No, I have to take steps. (Yaps and yaps and yaps and stops.) Hmm, tasty. He's giving me something? Because I was so great at barking? I know he was talking in his angry voice, but he also slipped me something, and usually he only ever does that when I've done something well. Hmm, that angry voice probably didn't mean a thing. After all, he often says things that don't match his body language, and that must be the case now. But I'd better try again to make sure. (Barks.) Indeed. I bark, and get something to eat. Fantastic. We stand here, it's boring, I bark and get something to eat. Wicked!
It's still a bit boring, but it's tasty anyway and gives me something to do. Hmm, I wonder if I can persuade him to slip me something every time I bark at him? I'll carry on doing it in future.

This situation is familiar to all dog-owners, if not from experience with oneself and one's own dog (because, naturally, we always do everything right, setting clear examples to our dogs at all times), then certainly with others. Strolling along to the car we meet our neighbour who has just started out on a walk with his dog. As an ambulance was parked outside the Joneses' house all morning, he launches into a long-winded account of all the in and outs of the morning's events – complete with all the facts he has gleaned from intensive training with various hospital soaps, of course. Now, as we and the neighbour are becoming quite the experts concerning Mrs Jones's medical history, the neighbour's dog is getting more and more agitated. Suddenly he barks, wags his tail and barks, whilst looking his owner straight in the eye. The neighbour raises his voice for a moment, perhaps gives the quadruped a clip on the nose, and continues talking to us as the dog calms down for a bit. Yet the peace does not last long, for just a few seconds later our conversation is once again brutally interrupted by the eardrum-bursting sound of the dog's voice, and this time, the barking knows no end. Our neighbour first gives it a go with cursing and the habitual, 'Stop it', used by every dog-owner again and again, even though no dog ever really apparently connects it with being quiet. So off we go with the stuffing and thereby brief quieting of the dog with treats, because scolding isn't working and it's very embarrassing for the biped that his dog is interrupting the chat so rudely and clearly has no intention to obey. This works until the dog has eaten the goodies, then a tentative yap resounds, and the owner's hand strays back into the pocket before another continuous round of yapping can ensue. Before long, the dog has been taught a new trick: bark if you want to get something good to eat. Not only that, but also the behaviour that we have thus made appetising for our four-legged friend can be extremely irritating; the dog gets the hang of it incredibly quickly before all else, because this yapping to get treats is rewarded as richly as desired behaviour is: sporadically. In the example above, the dog has learned that he gets treats when he barks at his biped.

In this case he was successful because his owner wanted to hush him up. The next time, when he is standing at the traffic lights with his biped and barks at him, they may be alone; the situation isn't so awkward for the human and the quadruped gets scolded and told to

shut up. A little while later, though, the dog gets a treat again, because his human – for whatever reason – wants to hush him up as quickly as possible. This way, on a sporadic basis, the quadruped receives affirmation that keeps making him try out this behaviour just to see if today is the 'jackpot' day.

Having a dog that pulls on the lead is not only a strain, but it can also make encounters with other dog-owners and their four-legged friends more problematic.

Danger

Whose Sofa is it anyway?

The way to do it

Never try to put a stop to the unwanted barking by means of treats, as you'll only achieve the opposite. It is preferable to ignore the barking in the first place (difficult, if not impossible, I know) or work purposefully on a cue to stop barking.

Still, we're only human and we all make mistakes. Forget it; who needs chats with other people anyway when a dog is around – and 'dissociation from other bipeds' is exactly the right thing for boosting a potential reputation for eccentricity. What's more, walkies belong to our dog and to our dog alone, and should be dignified accordingly. After all, our dog dignifies them: he focuses on us entirely during the walk, turns round to look at us at regular intervals of a few metres, reacts to every whispered cue and only runs away free when we allow him to do so. At this point, I would like to take a moment to smash the daydreams of many dog-owners who lose themselves in such visions as their four-legged friend shooing crows across a freshly sown field again and just keeping on going, despite calls and whistles of hurricane proportions. Well, at least he never runs off without being told to do so.

Or does he? Ask yourself that question in all honesty and I am sure that the majority of dog-owners will have to admit that their dogs run off as soon as the releasing click of the karabiner announces the end of 'lead time'. He may not shoot off as though the devil himself in cat's form were at his heels, but he generally trots away without thinking about whether he's meant to or not. This, too, has been instilled into him, because people rarely ensure that the quadruped only heads for the hills after getting permission first. People rarely get their dog to sit or stay first, release the karabiner, wait a moment before allowing their dog to take a look around. One can instil a certain degree of composure, and this would be the occasion to do it. When the dog pulls on the lead, sometimes your biggest wish above all else is to let this dratted animal off the lead at last. Nevertheless, the dog should learn that the opening of the karabiner does not equate with running off, because dogs that pull, in particular, will go flat out a few metres from the destination in order to get to the spot where they are freed from those restrictive fetters.

Humans are creatures of habit and generally put their dogs on the lead, and take them off again, at virtually the same spot, in the same field that they use every day to give their dogs a run. Within a short space of time, our four-legged friends have made a note of where you're going and what that means: freedom. As they are often more familiar with the route than we humans are, they also know exactly at what point it's really worth mobilising the traction forces. The dog looks forward to the imminent release of the lead, and this builds up to a tension in the dog that can be felt physically. The excitement speeds up the heartbeat, muscles and all senses are adjusted to the imminent opportunity to be allowed to enjoy freedom for a short time at least, the karabiner is released... and off we go! But what if the karabiner has just been released and a jogger pops up? The human snatches at the dog to put him back on the lead quickly, and the increased energy in the dog accumulates. When the jogger on the horizon turns out to be a class of schoolchildren on a hiking trip and the quadruped is therefore unable to go off the lead on this occasion, the dog's ebullience remains unchanged. Added to this is a good pinch of frustration. Dogs that are very calm by nature stash this energy away somewhere, while other quadrupeds need to release the stored energy whatever way they can, which in turn may lead to repeated tugging on the lead or, in extreme cases, to wild hollering at passing people, dogs or other creatures. This is no fun for either dog or human.

There are many more reasons for putting the dog on the lead, even though you've only released the karabiner seconds before. At moments like these, it is especially good to know that the dog is close by. However, things get problematic if he tends to accelerate to such an extent within just a few seconds that by the time you want him back he is already in the middle of the field with his head down a mouse hole, out of hearing. You should therefore make sure that the dog stays sitting or standing still after the karabiner has been released until he gets the cue 'Run' (or whatever your choice of word may be).

Whose Sofa is it anyway?

Oh, these impossible bipeds!

To prevent too much tension from building up in him, you can sporadically practise putting the dog on the lead and taking him off again on different walks without letting him run off. This way, the clicking of the released karabiner will not turn into an automatic and self-contained cue for, 'Run away! You're no longer under my control.' This is a simple exercise that will – hopefully – have a big effect.

Why tyranny is fun

There are heaps of dogs that terrorise their family and people around them and occasionally conduct themselves like born tyrants. However, very few quadrupeds are born with the 'tyrant' gene; rather, they are forced into this role.

Typical problems that all dog-owners have at least heard about because they happened to acquaintances (never to themselves, naturally) include:

Problem number 1:
The dog takes possession of the sofa.

Problem number 2:
The dog jumps up at strangers.

Problem number 3:
The dog keeps pulling on the lead.

Problem number 4:
The dog cannot be left on his own.

Eye to eye. It can be pretty impressive when big dogs jump up at people!

Who's the king of the sofa? Things get really interesting when there's no room left for the human.

Problem number 1: Sofa possession

To be a very welcome guest everywhere and at all times with a well-behaved quadruped; to be able to take one's dog along to wherever it may be – to the city centre for some shopping, the restaurant or hotel, where he lies down calmly and takes in the other diners' gazes as they admire his composure; or on visits to family or friends; our dog is with us everywhere, and with chests puffed out with pride we gladly accept the appreciative comments from the rest of humanity; this is the absolute dream of many dog-owners. Unfortunately, the reality often looks different.

Sammy may have made himself unpopular with friends and family because, clean or not, after a brief exploratory tour of the unknown home, he settles down nice and comfortably on the sofa. It is a matter of total indifference to him whether this is a robust, washable leather sofa or a white Italian designer couch. Most dogs, though, have exquisite taste and, given the choice between a designer sofa and a washable cover, tend to go for the fancy furniture. Hurray for third-party pet liability insurance, without which many dog-owners would already be on the brink of ruin and taking one step closer to the abyss with every visit to friends and family.

Before you know it, you're suddenly expressly being asked to appear – if you're invited at all – without your dog when summoned into the presence of dogless people (whose numbers are dwindling in any case). At this point I'd like to mention that a potential though subtle shift in friend circles may occur in dog-owner's life. Dogless acquaintances switch to friendships with dog-owners who are not going to bring in huge quantities of dog-hair and dirt because their dogs have a clean track record. It is therefore all the more embarrassing when, in the presence of non-dog people, the beloved quadruped suddenly appears to have forgotten all propriety and, even after several requests, refuses to get down off the dog-hair-free, light-beige corner sofa. The good dog-owner thinks up another ruse and claims firmly that he has no idea what's got into his dog, because he never does it otherwise. The sour look from mother-in-law, first at our quadruped (who unfortunately discovered the cake and is now also slobbering all over the furniture), and then straight at our walkies-friendly, but rather unflattering, walking boots is a clear indication that all excuses here will be in vain and we and our dog should not make our visit too long.

All the way home we ask ourselves what could be the reason why we failed to make it clear to our dog, in a word, that he must sit on the floor, and that the sofa is for humans only.

This is a matter of total indifference to our dog. He has done everything the way he's learned it and cannot understand why the visit to that beautifully clean house was so stressful, or why so much animosity was in the air. At home, after all, he is always allowed to lie on the couch and nobody grumbles, so why should this be undesirable somewhere else? If, back home, he is allowed to take possession of sofa, armchair and bed to his heart's desire, to sleep or get cuddles, this surely

From the dog's point of view, rules that we set up at home apply in all places. Therefore, sleep in bed once, sleep in bed always, no matter where.

26

applies at all times. So how is he meant to tell that it is allowed at home, but that a whole world crumbles in other people's homes or hotel rooms if he merely sets one foot on the furniture?

We need to tie another knot in our handkerchiefs here: rules that we set up at home apply everywhere. This also goes for permission given to our four-legged friends to lie down wherever and whenever they like. If you ban your dog from making himself at home any place and any time, he will heed this ban at all times and in all places. But most dog-people reckon it's perfectly fine for their dog to flop down next to them on the sofa. After all, this a much better way to cuddle up and conduct that socially important game of trust, grooming. Essentially, there can be no objections to this either, because contrary to long-established notions, we are not bringing up our dog to be dominant if he is allowed to occupy elevated positions. Just one thing needs to be clear at all times: when we ask him to make room for us, there are no arguments. He pushes off and we sit down.

The way to do it

Now, to make it easier for our dog to pick the right place in unknown surroundings, from the day he moves in we can establish that he is only permitted to lie on the spot on the sofa or bed where a certain (soon to be his) blanket is spread out. Every time he fails to lie down on his blanket, we send him to it so that this association is quickly formed in the quadruped's mind: I am only allowed to lie down where this soft thing is, and I'll be left in peace.

We can save the day on visits to mother-in-law by laying out the dog's blanket in one corner of the room and allowing our four-legged friend to make himself at home on it without shedding all his hairs on the animal-hair-free, hence sweet-smelling divan.

27

Problem number 2:
Jumping up

Many people will recognise this problem, either because they have a dog that is so delighted to see other bipeds that his fondest wish is to knock them over, or because they have had to suppress an attack of maniacal proportions after a visit to friends with dogs has resulted in yet another visit to the dry cleaner.

Like nearly all problems later in life, jumping up has its origins in puppyhood. Little fur-balls are extraordinarily cute, and it's impossible for most people to be angry with a clumsy little canine baby when it tries to clamber up the trouser-legs of every human being to get to the person's face. With every encounter, puppies' immediate intention is to appease the giant bipeds, to nuzzle up to them and prove how innocent and delightful small dogs are. Their additional aim is to make sure that nobody ever does them any harm. Most bipeds that belong a puppy's social circle take painstaking care to bend down to the little chap to greet him so that he doesn't need to jump up. This is laudable and theoretically a promising method, if it weren't for all the other people that one encounters every single day.

Most of humanity is totally obsessed with comical little puppies and simply cannot resist talking to the pretty fur-balls in baby language and hugging them as the canine infants jump up gleefully at the nice bipeds to get even closer to them. If it is summer and the little fur-bundles are clean and dry, even strangers are happy to turn a blind eye because the little one is 'just so cute'.

So what's instilled into the canine infant is: I have no need to jump up at my bipeds, because we find other ways to greet each other. But all other humans think it's great when I say a really big hello to them. The few exceptions where I am not allowed to jump up are surely not the general rule, and you've just got to give it a go with all bipeds.

Ultimately, the droll little quadruped that turns everybody's head grows into a great big dog that – whether it's raining and he has muddy paws or he is freshly bathed and clean – tries to greet everybody who even gives him a friendly look by jumping up.

We can imagine how thrilled other people are going to be when the former little puppy turns into a fully-grown male mastiff. With a bit of luck the only person we're putting off is mother-in-law, but it is more likely that

It's good when a dog has learned not to jump up at people. This quadruped could be the cause of some serious cleaning bills.

a whole lot of bother is in store for the bipeds belonging to the notorious jumper-upper.

Being responsible dog-owners who are going to be called to account for everything our dog ever gets up to – and who will have to bear the cleaning costs for Chanel suits ruined by muddy paws – we need to ensure right from the start that the people around us play to our rules. This includes asking everybody who wants to hug our dog to bend down to him and only say hello to him once he's sitting down. This way, the quadruped will very soon learn that it is worth his while to sit down in front of new people straight away and that jumping up will not get him anywhere.

The way to do it

So what's to do? Take vigorous action! And that applies to all people who really need to touch, hug and say hello to our dog because he's just so cute.

Whose Sofa is it anyway?

Problem number 3:
Pulling on the lead

If having the dog pull on the lead were the highest aspiration of dog training, about 80 per cent of all dog-owners would earn a distinction.

From the chihuahua to the mastiff, they can be seen and heard: those rasping and panting dogs that hang on the lead with all their strength to get further and further ahead and closer and closer to an unseen, but clearly extremely important destination, and, above all else, be the first one there.

At the other end of the line dangles a usually desperate biped, who has either

'Done it! I'm finally free of the bothersome other end of the lead.

already given up and is assuming the most absurd postures in order to avoid (or at least cushion) long-term spinal damage, or a person who has not given up yet and is screaming at his quadruped every few seconds that he really shouldn't pull like that. However, this plea is never heeded, for pulling dogs are notorious for appearing to be deaf to such requests.

Besides these, there are those dog-owners who sporadically perform the lead exercises they learned sometime in the past and change direction like a crazed thing, only to continue on their way filled with bitterness after the tenth time and allow the dog to keep pulling. All the same, at least an attempt has been made to teach the dog the thing with the slack lead, and tomorrow is another day.

Incidentally, at the age of about ten years most dogs no longer have sufficient strength to leap rigorously into action as draught animals, so there is hope.

Whereas the human knows that the lead is sometimes a necessary evil to keep the dog close by, for the freedom-loving dog it is a utensil that

Get two and four-legged colleagues from the dog school to come outside and practise all the things that make a dog sociable. (Photo: Lamozik)

Oh, these impossible bipeds!

ought to be banned outright. The tugging on the collar makes it difficult to perform undisturbed sniffing at any desired point, let alone shooting off to chase birds or other wild animals. The lead totally prevents the dog of the world from reaching his destination via the fastest and shortest possible route.

There are many places where the dog needs to be on the lead. Therefore, there is no getting around some good lead practice. (Photo: Slawik)

Even puppies soon work out that lead and collar are totally unnecessary. Staying put and being stubborn are futile, as one is only dragged along behind. This funny rope ties a dog to the human and means that, from now on, this human determines direction and speed.

A dog grasps incredibly quickly that we bipeds, compared with him, have totally underdeveloped sensory organs. On walks, we never steer towards the correct – the best-smelling – point, and we only ever creep along instead of trotting through the countryside at a decent pace. Therefore, once a dog has learned that the stupid rope around his neck means exploring the world beyond the front garden, it only remains for him to assert his will on the lead and drag the human behind him in order to find the attractive and most noteworthy points in the surroundings at a decent pace. So, there is pulling, snuffling, running back, more snuffling, running forward and pulling in the process – continuously.

33

After all, the lead not only means restriction.

No: it also means the freedom to take an exploratory sniff around, discover the world and perhaps make a few friends.

The whole wide world is waiting to be conquered. You just need to be fast enough to experience it all. But because the biped who is dangling behind on the lead somewhere is advancing so slowly, the dog really goes flat out. After all, there's a crazy amount to be discovered, and things really need to get going before there's any risk of missing out on the best. So up we get. The main thing is to move forward, towards a defined destination. Though the pulling on the throat squashes the larynx, the inevitable lack of oxygen also increases the release of adrenalin, which in turn leads to a kind of euphoria. This is a vicious circle that the human really should prevent from day one.

But what is the best method if one is not lucky enough to be accompanied by a dog that, without needing to be asked twice, recognises that the idea is to let the lead remain slack?

Dogs that pull on the lead are one of the most extensive topics of conversation at dog schools. The biggest problem is that lead training requires a lot of consistency and, above all, can be lengthy. For most people it is too much effort. They very soon give up and just live with their dog permanently pulling on the lead (which is less dramatic and strenuous with a dog weighing three kilos than it is with a fifty-kilo quadruped).

The flourishing pet accessories market offers a multitude of aids that despairing but willing dog-owners can treat themselves to. Most of them guarantee effectiveness, but very few of them can really be recommended. To everybody who leads his dog on a spiked collar or strangling device, I have one thing to say: try putting it on yourself and then straining on a lead. I hope that you've hung on to the receipt so you can change the item for a soft leather collar or, even better, a chest harness straight away. Yet if we are not meant to use instruments of torment, how can we ensure that the quadruped spends at least the majority of his time on the lead not tugging and concentrating on building up his muscled chest?

There are various options, but no matter what method you go for, the important thing is that there are no exceptions and you must be consistent at all times and in all places, because a step backwards is taken every time the dog is allowed to pull.

The way to do it

Method number 1:
As soon as the dog starts pulling, change direction. If he lets the lead remain slack, he gets verbal praise or a treat.

Method number 2:
If the dog strains on the lead, draw him aside gently so that he loses sight of his destination. If he proceeds as desired, let him know that that's exactly the right thing to do.

Method number 3:
The quadruped is led on a lead at least three metres long and is stopped whenever he's about to reach the end of the lead, so that he learns that his radius is limited.

Method number 4:
People who work with a clicker can turn walks on the lead into clicker sessions where the dog gets a click every time he walks alongside them. On other hand, sometimes this can produce a dog that only ever walks to heel, which can also get a bit annoying in the long term. Therefore, make sure that you click not for walking to heel, but for not pulling.

There are many more methods to stop your dog mutating from a canine into a tugging shire horse, but the methods mentioned above are the usual ones and, if they are applied correctly and consistently, ought to be successful.

One more tip:

As you don't always have time and leisure for a training session straight after leaving the house with the dog on the lead, start enabling the dog to differentiate between pulling that is allowed and pulling that is not. For example, you can put a chest harness on the dog if you don't want to train and he can really go for it with the straining (it is also not as bad for the dog's neck vertebrae as a collar), whereas he is not permitted to pull under any circumstances when wearing the collar.

Problem number 4:
Being unable to be left alone

'My dog yowls so terribly every time I leave the house. He can't stay on his own for five minutes before the neighbours start wanting to call the police. It can't go on like this.' This is more or less the formulation of a problem repeated every few minutes around the world, for which people generally have themselves to blame. These days, a dog has to be able to be alone for a few hours without delighting an entire neighbourhood with the piercing sounds of his wretchedly resounding tale of suffering. However, first he needs to learn how to stay on his own at all.

When a dog enters his new family, no matter whether he is already a fully grown quadruped or a puppy, he is in uncertain territory. He finds himself in new surroundings, all that was familiar to him has suddenly given way and he is completely alone in a new world where he does not yet know the rules.

First of all, our task is to show him that he can trust his new humans and that he will get support and guidance in his unknown surroundings to make it as easy as possible for him to settle in. As long as they treat him right, after only a few days the quadruped's humans have become the centre of his world in which he can trust blindly, and who will never let him down.

However, there then comes the moment when the door shuts, the humans, his support and comfort, disappear and leave him behind. His world no longer makes sense to him.

Everything that's important and dear to him in life is leaving him behind. Completely alone. How is he meant to

know what's coming next? What's going to happen? Fears and panic are terrible emotions, and these are precisely what he's experiencing now, and the only thing that might just help him is to call out, to scream at high volume for his pack, which must stand together at all times so that it can face up to all the horrors of the world. Louder and louder all the time, until finally, maybe after some hours, the door is opened again and the beaming sun of his world rises again. So, it was a help then; his loud shouting had the result that his human appeared again, to stand by his side. In short, from the dog's point of view, loud screaming helps to put an end to the loneliness.

The way to do it

A dog must be gradually made accustomed to staying on his own. He has to learn that it is not a bad thing if we leave the house without him, because we will come back to him. The dog has to learn that he can trust us in every situation, that we will not leave him behind and that he need not fear that he will die a lonely death.

Initially, only leave the house or apartment for a short time, shut the door and come back straight away. Then start with a few minutes and prolong the duration step by step.

However, it is important never to go back in when the dog is barking.

37

He must not form this association: I scream, therefore my human comes straight back to me. Yet this is exactly what many dog-owners do, thus instilling into the dog the habit of yapping his heart out whenever he's alone.

Most dogs very quickly learn how to stay on their own for quite a while. If the quadruped is kept sufficiently occupied, there is a chance that the human may just return to a habitat that still looks inhabitable and not as though it has just been torn apart by a horde of wild lions. In many cases, dogs that give full vent to their destructive fury as soon as they are alone have never learned how to stay on their own. They express their fear by busying themselves with something that distracts them, and this usually does not comply with human notions of breaking down fear or frustration.

Instead of swearing at the dog in such cases, one should think up a solution and work on the problem: for example, by providing a room for him to stay in where he can do no damage and giving him a whole range of chewy items to play with. (Alternatively, you can also gradually get the dog used to a dog carrier.)

However, work on the staying alone. Train the dog in slow phases, and never lose your patience. A dog loves his human and he does not want to be separated from him or her. We're the ones to blame, not our dogs, because we haven't conveyed enough trust and security to them.

There are an infinite number of other problems that a dog-owner will need to face as the years go by. However, even going by the four named above, one thing is very clear: in everything that we expect from our pets, we must set up clear rules that apply at all times. The dog is unable to decide when the moment has come to do something differently to the way he is otherwise permitted or asked to do it. Whatever we expect from our dog must be valid at all times. No matter whether we are trying to teach him never, ever to pull on the lead, whether we want him to learn never to jump up at a person or not to jump on to every sofa, we are responsible for teaching him to follow these rules consistently.

It is a mistake to assume that the dog knows exactly when he's permitted to do something and when he is not. We make it incredibly difficult for ourselves and our dog when we allow him to pull just for once because we're not in the mood for training today. How is the dog supposed to know that actually he must never pull, but on Mondays, Wednesdays and Sundays we have

Even with a face like this, this dog has learned that it is not the end of the world if he has to stay on his own.

such stressful days that we have no leisure to do lead training? How is the quadruped meant to learn to distinguish between Mrs Smith, who doesn't mind at all when Trixie jumps up at her, and Mr Jones, who threatens to send the public health authorities after us when a somewhat impetuous dog 'attacks' him? From our dog's point of view, everybody in the world could be a Mrs Smith.

Above all, a dog cannot know that not all sofas on this planet are there solely for lying on if he is always allowed to do it at home. He cannot know that there is a difference between our furniture – covered up and dog-friendly – and the spotlessly clean beds of a four-star hotel. Every time, we need to see things from the quadruped's angle and ask ourselves what we really expect, finally gearing our actions towards this expectation and thus creating one or two fewer problems.

All pretty easy really, isn't it?

Chewing is a distraction!

Napoleons are created, not born

There are many, many dogs that go crazy when they see the faintest flicker of another dog on the horizon. They bark, they growl, they clamour. They show the whole world that they are the kings before whom the whole canine world must bow. In their moments of terror, they quickly forget the fact that they soon cease these carryings-on when they are off the lead and far away from the human.

For the other end of the lead, which after all is doing the holding, frenzies like this are terribly unpleasant. From pleas to the quadruped to finally shut up, through yelling (and therefore, from the dog's point of view, joining in to scare off the others), to immediate escape through the undergrowth, anything goes. No matter what reaction the dog's behaviour inspires in the biped, it is always accompanied by the question: why does it have to be my dog?

Let's take a look at a potential transformation into a canine Napoleon by the example of Puff, the terrier. (Note: the following applies not only for terriers, but equally for every breed. The principle is always the same.)

There can be various motives for threatening and growling.

Naturally, doting dog parents only want the best for their Puff, and the best upbringing begins with the best socialisation. Therefore, Puff gets to know many things in his surroundings, and some of them frighten him a little bit. Of course, this is not want his dog parents want, and they certainly do not want anything bad to happen to him. What is more, Puff is so much smaller and cuddlier than all other dogs in the world, so he is always brought into safety whenever his human companions get the notion that God's wrath could hammer down on him imminently if they don't take real care. This wrath frequently manifests itself in the form of big, mean-looking dogs. Puff's

41

Oh, these impossible bipeds!

bipeds are unconscious of the fact that these dogs are often really nice and harmless and are only lumbered with being the wrong colour or size. They only know one thing: our little one must not undergo any unpleasant experiences because otherwise he will disappear, in one gulp, down the big dog's throat, never to be seen again. So, because you can't be too sure, they prefer to pick up their innocent little lamb during encounters with big dogs.

For Puff, this is fantastic. Whereas previously, he merely noticed that an older, bigger dog was coming towards him, to whom respect was due purely because of the size difference, in an instant he has grown from a dwarf into a giant.

The dog's logical conclusion is:

I, tiny mite Puff, am theoretically untouchable, because I grow to many times my physical size when other dogs approach.
What's more, my humans carry on talking loudly to me, which probably means that the other quadrupeds need to be scolded at from above, to drive them away.
To the others, I am the master, descending from the sky.

Keep a watchful eye on the little dog, but it is preferable not to pick him up.
(Photo: Fritschy)

The more often he (in his view) drives away other dogs by means of furious yapping from his owner's arm, the more reinforced this behaviour becomes, so that Puff internalises it to such an extent that he soon begins to give voice to his giant ego from the ground, no matter how big or small the other dog is. After all, he has learned that he can – indeed, is expected to – scold away with impunity.

Don't bring up a Napoleon. Even little dogs with big courage can face down their man.

This way, one brings up one's very own Napoleon that never had the chance to recognise his own size and learn sociable behaviour. This is a 'method' frequently applied by dog parents to mis-train their dog. With the best of intentions, people try to enable the dog to live a good (and, above all, long) life, and people rarely picture the consequences of not treating him or letting him grow up like a dog. Certainly, it is not easy to find the ideal middle ground between over-anxiousness and thoughtlessness, but a few scratches are part of growing up, not only for children, but also dogs.

It goes without saying that this in no way means that one's dog must be left to cope with difficult situations everywhere and at all times. Not every unknown dog is able to teach one's own dog good social behaviour; after all, we do not even know whether this unknown dog is sociable at all. But finding well-socialised dogs is, after all, a task that we, as dog parents, should take on by talking to other dog-owners, for example, and observing their dogs, or attending dog schools, even before getting a puppy, and giving some thought as to whether this puppy class may be the right one.

We've been doing it this way for 30 years

More than once during our lifetime and activity as dog-owners, we come across him: the original know-it-all dog-owner. He lurks on walks, in inner cities, at the vet's or in restaurants that we visit with our quadruped – and always when things are not going quite so well: when Fido growls at Puff at the vet's because he's giving him a funny look, or when Molly flashes her bright white teeth at the Labrador she meets on a walk.

The know-it-all dog-owner

In such situations, the average dog-owner will either think to murmur 'Sorry' and pull the dog away or otherwise distract him, to keep the damage as slight as possible. Yet before you know it and have escaped from the firing line and back into your own thoughts, you are halted by a carping voice that immediately begins to lecture in a schoolmasterly tone on how you could do it differently and better with Fido or Molly. The original

know-it-all dog-owner is waiting at all times and in all places with a free lesson on the subject of bringing up dogs.

You really have to take drastic measures now.

For example, if you encounter him on a walk during which your Fido barks at his dog, you immediately receive the basic lecture in matters of obedience training.

The long-winded expositions mostly start with: 'You really need to take drastic measures now; otherwise, it will get worse and worse.' Somewhere during the monologue about taking drastic measures, dominance and 'not putting up with it', the lecture is bound to contain the words: 'I know what I'm talking about; I have had dogs for thirty years.' This bit is delivered with a chest puffed out with pride and in the tone of total conviction that the knowledge acquired thirty years ago is still valid and above all, still valid for absolutely every dog. After all, individuality is hopelessly overrated.

The old-school supporter has successfully managed to circumvent all findings about learning behaviour and all animal protection laws, and is still trying to convert the poor souls who obviously don't have the upper hand over their quadrupeds. Unfortunately, not only can these practices be encountered in private households, but also there are more and more dog schools or clubs that teach that the only way to make a dog obey is to break his will.

'Positions and heel!'

A few years ago, when I was looking for a dog club where I could work in the company of other dogs with my totally psychologically deranged rescue dog, my search also took me to a club's training session in the neighbouring town.

As I was still naive in canine matters, and as the words 'friend' and 'dog' popped up in the club's name, I went to the introductory afternoon with a good feeling. No doubt about it, the welcome was very pleasant, and after I had explained the various problems with my dog it was very soon pronounced that 'it would certainly be possible to beat that out of her'. I should have become suspicious there and then as, in retrospect, that word beat spoke volumes. Fortunately for me (and especially for my dog), I turned down the offer to join in with the lesson that was currently taking place, thanked them and sat down at the edge of the training ground to watch at leisure. Shortly afterwards the first human/dog teams appeared and walked on to the ground, while the people who had come with these teams joined me at the edge to watch their partners during the training.

The good thing about this group, I thought, was that it was very mixed: from the medium-sized mongrel, through a Dalmatian to the Rottweiler, almost everything was represented. However, I was concerned that every one of these dogs was wearing a spiked collar.

There was another new person there besides me, an older lady with an incredibly sweet Spitz mongrel that looked around in joyous expectation and simply worshipped her owner. As the owner explained, her Lara was lacking in obedience and was here to learn it. She joined the lesson with Lara immediately and went up to the couples on the training ground.

And then he arrived – the trainer. The scene looked so surreal to me that I could have choked on my hearty laughter. Out of the clubhouse came a man who gave the impression that he had just leapt directly out of a cheap action film: hair shaved to a few millimetres, a black combat uniform and black

Two-legged dog parents take on a task that entails responsibilities when they bring a puppy home.

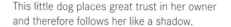
This little dog places great trust in her owner and therefore follows her like a shadow.

and set off. It was a piteous sight: dragging and jerking on the lead if the dog advanced just one centimetre too far. The unhappy looks on the dogs' faces, the tails between the legs – no joy in the teamwork could be seen in a single one of the dogs, only uncertainty and fear about when the next painful jerk, the next totally unpredictable bawl-out would come. Only Lara ran joyously alongside her owner and gazed at her adoringly. All right, her walking to heel was not perfect but she was visibly enjoying this shared activity. Enjoyment – on his dog-training ground? The sergeant (sorry, trainer) could not let that one pass. He strode up to Lara and owner, grabbed the lead and went for it: dragged the distressed dog behind him, tore at the lead like a crazed man in order to keep her to heel, and shrieked at the dog every five seconds to walk to 'heel'. When he pressed the lead back into the hand of Lara's horrified owner, the only thing a totally distressed Lara could think of was a quick exit and an escape from the hell that had just revealed itself to her. But that was not to be. The trainer took Lara's owner to task: the dog was dominant and, from

leather boots. Added to this, a fierce expression and, unfortunately, the corresponding voice and mood.

So, he strode into the middle of the training ground and hollered 'Positions and heel!' across the ground in a blood-curdling voice. In an instant the participants positioned themselves in a row

Whose Sofa is it anyway?

now on, needed to be led on a spiked collar at all times. What is more, would the owner finally adopt another tone, she had been too gentle up to now. Unfortunately, this story went even further: I heard a woman whose husband had completed the training with the family Dalmatian telling another spectator in a chatty tone that the dog always hid behind the couch as soon as they got out the spiked collar.

At that moment, that was definitely that for me. I railed against such training methods under my breath, made my way back to my car as quickly as possible and fled back into the enlightened age, into a world where dog-friendly training had already been heard of. I frequently can't help thinking about Lara, a friendly dog that loved her owner and that had perhaps been robbed of her trust in her family forever, just because of a lack of obedience.

Unfortunately, there are still many dog-owners who believe that violence and yelling are the only way to teach a dog anything. Now, if these people come across a dog that has just picked up on how to defend himself against the blunderings, whether it be out of fear or because he is fed up of the endless provocations, we have a dog that is potentially unpredictable. Things can end unhappily for the dog, especially if he defends himself by biting.

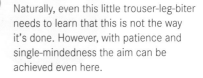

Naturally, even this little trouser-leg-biter needs to learn that this is not the way it's done. However, with patience and single-mindedness the aim can be achieved even here.

49

Violence has no place in the upbringing of animals. Breaking an animal's will to make it submissive is one of the lowest imaginable mechanisms, and only humans are capable of it. Patience, single-mindedness and simple, clear language are the manual tools with which we succeed in turning our quadruped into an obedient companion.

Place yourself in the situation of dogs that are expected, on the basis of pain, to learn what walking to heel means. The only thing the dog ever notices is that the pain is inflicted at apparently deliberately chosen intervals, and indeed by the person in whom he trusts. He does not know why this pain comes, and tries to find to trigger. Is it the other dog coming towards him? Is there always pain then? Is it painful whenever another biped comes? Or perhaps whenever he looks at a child? The requirement that he must walk directly alongside his owner in order not to feel pain is an extremely abstract piece of learning for a quadruped, which in this case means lots and lots of pain before the dog may just be able to understand it.

If you encounter one of these incorrigible people who are still, as far as training is concerned, living in the 1950s, you are best advised to clear off with your dog as fast as possible.

You will never get back the time that these people steal from you and your dog in order to impart antiquated and pet-tormenting words of wisdom, and this time can put to better use. You can, for example, work on 'Lie down' and 'Stay' with a bit of patience and some treats, or maybe work on walking on the lead.

Fortunately, the negative example described above is an extreme exception. Of course, this doesn't go on in all dog clubs and dog schools; there are more and more positive examples to the contrary.

Bringing up a dog with love and enthusiasm will lead to an enduring relationship. Violence is taboo. (Photo: Slawik)

Ancient wisdom and our search for a better reality

This chapter deals with one of the loveliest occupations that we dog-owners pursue day after day: the invention of any excuses to apologise for the rude habits of our beloved quadruped. Yet the shocking thing is not that we make constant efforts to have our dog appear in the best light, but more that we ourselves often really believe what we are saying. This then results in the oft-cited and now standard words of the type: 'He's never done that before,' or (also popularly used time after time), 'He only wants to play.'

Dogs sometimes have a tendency to do precisely what they are not allowed to do.

I admit that even I have used one or the other excuse because no hole appeared in the ground to swallow me and my blushes up after yet another embarrassing canine situation.

Even though every dog-owner has had to excuse his or dog in an embarrassing situation at some point, one day some dog-owners will have successfully suppressed those dark days and feel that they are free of all blame. Yet even those who live with perfectly trained or simply thoroughly nice dogs are bound to have had the pleasure of encountering us self-conscious dog-owners who are never embarrassed to give excuses.

Why do we believe that we need to excuse our pets' behaviour?

Can it perhaps have something to do with the ancient 'wisdom' that we dog-owners have all heard before and that many people still believe is the benchmark for training dogs?

What situations are typically the ones in which popular sayings (which can, even now, still be obtained printed on t-shirts, bags and other accessories) are applied? A brief foray into the world of training myths and splendid excuses may perhaps explain it.

No digging

But I have heard...

They are lurking everywhere, and there is no hiding from them: the people who make a comment about everything, who simply know it all better than we do, whether they are trying to explain how to pack a suitcase correctly or whether they meet us on a walk and loudly impart their wisdom in all things dog-training – and whether we want to know it or not.

Interestingly, it is always the same stories that the innocuous walker and his dog are forced to hear. Well-worn and long since disproved theories are expounded in a manner worthy of a local bar room bore, whether it is the 'They'll sort it out among themselves' theory that's being discussed, or the popular and above all antiquated house-training method that goes: 'Rub the puppy's nose in his business' – a cruel punishment for a quadruped with such a highly developed sense of smell as our dogs. However, I'm particularly tickled personally by the widely spread myth concerning the perennial 'puppy protection'.

It would certainly be worth inventing a specific research field for finding out where the theories come from.

One thing is certain, though, that these theories, just like urban myths, spread further and further and nobody knows precisely where he or she has actually heard whatever it is that's being passed on, but everybody knows that they 'heard somewhere that...'

As a run-of-the-mill dog-owner, you generally hear these theories on relaxed walks where you encounter other dog-owners. Now, we dog-owners are sociable folk and are generally not disinclined to immerse ourselves in a pleasant chat with other dog-owners. In the ideal case, the conversation starts because the respective quadrupeds have just made friends and start to play about boisterously. In the rather less ideal case, you exchange addresses because the quadrupeds have decided to test their respective strengths. You often have this case when two dogs come across each other, demonstrating just from their posture that they are not willing simply to pursue their ways past each other calmly and peacefully, and one of the two dog-owners calls to the other: 'Don't worry, they'll sort it out between them!' In most cases a fight has broken out before the sentence is finished. Why some people are so deliberately keen on their dog getting caught in scraps will always be a puzzle to me. There may well

'I don't normally do this – honest!'
(Photo: Kuhn)

be minor regular conflicts within a pack, but when total canine strangers that do not live together, and also do not generally meet each other regularly, approach each other in anticipation of aggression (recognisable by the crouching posture, frequently accompanied by raised hackles and tail held high, along with a fixing stare), you should not trust that the matter will see a rapid and above all entirely blood-free conclusion.

What is learned by a dog that is allowed to torment at all times and in all places? If he is generally the stronger one in a fight, then he learns that mobbing is a pretty cool thing that one ought to repeat as often as possible, because after all it's a boost to the doggy ego. If he is often the underdog, then this only shows him that all other dogs are stupid and his biped is incapable of keeping a proper eye on him.

Both cases are going to entail problems in that both the strong one and the underdog will lose no time in ensuring that relaxed walks in total peace and quiet are a thing of the past as soon as another dog is in sight. The strong one wants to show the other one who lays down the rules here, while the weak one wants to

make it clear even from a distance that one is ill-advised to come too close. Here we have it: they do indeed sort it out between themselves, but the consequences that must be borne after such nearly always avoidable clashes are really not worth it.

The subject of house-training also provides room for an endless number of theories on how to do it. If you stand in the middle of a group of grown people who each call a puppy their own, the topic will be so hotly debated that your head will soon be buzzing.

When a group like this is assembled, it won't be long before the question, 'And how do you do your house-training?' is thrown into the ring –

As a dog-owner, you must keep a close eye on situations like these and intervene in emergencies. (Photo: Röder)

and everyone will jump on to it, like a horde of crows on to road kill. The reason why this topic is so popular is because everybody has something to say. After all, all new dog parents have to go through this and are always willing to exchange their experiences. In terms of eagerness to communicate, puppy groups aren't in the least bit different from parent groups at nursery school.

House-training

Let me continue by clearing away the customary house-training methods that are unfortunately still in use.

Error 1:

Rubbing the dog's nose in it and exclaiming, 'Hey!'

I already gave a brief hint at the start of this chapter on what should be thought of this method. Although still widespread ('The neighbour of a friend of a friend had a dog ten years ago, and he said that was the way to do it'), the dipping of a little clean canine infant into his own doings belongs right at the back of the closet of antiquated training methods. The dog may well find it very unpleasant, but the learning effect will remain at zero. He doesn't know what he has done wrong, and he doesn't get shown what he's expected to do differently and better.

Tip: Essentially, one thing must be remembered on the subject of punishment: it should always be used after careful consideration and in small doses and must never concern absolutely natural, dog-typical behaviour. However, if you are still determined to tell off your quadruped for something, then this must happen straight away (within the first five seconds after the misdemeanour, preferably still during the undesired behaviour).

Error 2:

Whacking the puppy with a newspaper on finding the doings indoors.

This seems to be the most popular method, at least if the many conversations that I have been privileged to hear in the widest variety of puppy groups can be believed. For a reason that remains a mystery to me, human beings are constantly at pains to thrash about with objects. Could it be that this is a relic of the stone age when, armed with cudgels, we tried to banish sabre-toothed tigers from our caves (or house-train them – who's to know)?

The thing here is that apart from the fact that we cruelly shake the primal sense of trust with which the little dog tumbled into this world and that he unwaveringly places in us when we whack him one on the bottom with the newspaper, this method has no effect. As described above, the timespan in this case between the doing of the business and the punishment is far too long for the dog to understand that he's getting whacked for peeing in the hall. To him, this is just yet another

None of these puppies has been house-trained yet.
There is much debate on the best way to do it.

indication of the incompetence and unpredictability of the human, who clobbers him out of the blue. How is a canine infant meant to develop in such a way that he has faith in his biped's dependability?

He needs to know that his owner is a totally supreme pack leader who does the right thing in every situation. Quite apart from all this, why should one punish an animal for answering a call of nature? When things take a nosedive (but preferably not the dog into his own doings), the person is to blame for not taking care again and failing to show the dog an alternative place to do it in time.

Error 3:

I find the following way to house-train a puppy absolutely appalling. This story was told to me by a participant in one of my young-dog classes. Another trainer had advised her to do it this and no other way.

The little puppy is tied to the table on a short one-metre line and receives neither food nor water if nobody has time to look after him. As puppies do not dirty their beds, he does not soil the apartment until he is taken outside. However, if he fouls this place he is beaten so that he gets the message that this is undesirable.

Only humans can be this cruel. Just imagine the little mite attached to a line that provides him with no freedom of movement for hours on end, suffering from hunger and thirst and desperately trying to hold it in until it's impossible. Then he is overjoyed because his beloved human finally comes back to liberate him, and he only gets beaten. I probably do not need to spend too long explaining why this dog felt absolutely no loyalty towards his owner and, during the lesson, clung on to every other person but did not voluntarily run up to her. Trust had not only been shaken to its foundations, but completely destroyed so that ultimately the only option was to give the dog away to a new family. Despite many trust-building exercises, the puppy hid behind me at every lesson every time his owner called him in a friendly voice and enticed him with treats. The wound ran too deep for it to be possible to stitch it up and turn the two of them into a team where they could rely on each other one hundred per cent in every situation.

The rewarding of desired behaviour can help ensure that undesired behaviour does not occur in the first place and hence will not require punishment.

The way to do it

Teaching a young dog that he is only allowed to do his business outside is one of the simplest exercises on the long road of upbringing. All it takes is a person who pays close attention and reacts quickly, and the rest will soon follow by itself. Basically, puppies need to go out very soon after eating or drinking. It's already high time when they turn round in a sheltered spot conspicuously often or sniff about there and are already starting to wriggle their little bodies. Ideally, one picks up the canine infant swiftly (remember: one hand goes under the little doggy bottom) and goes to a spot where he can relieve himself in peace. Friendly words as a reward show him that peeing outside is super. After several repetitions, the puppy very soon understands that he should go to the door through which he is always carried outside whenever it's time to answer the call of nature. Nevertheless, the odd boo-boo will occur occasionally. If you find a puddle or even a pile, clean it away without comment and make a mental note to pay better attention from now on.

Keeping a close eye on the puppy is an essential requirement for house-training. This little chap has just relieved himself and is now playing merrily out of doors.

Caution! Puppy protection is a myth.

Puppy protection

One topic that is familiar to anybody who has ever owned a puppy is puppy protection. I am in possession of a formidable collection of dog books on the widest variety of subjects, and never have I encountered in any of these books the theory that, because he is under puppy protection, a puppy can be let loose in the dog world without reservations.

Whatever the origins of this myth may be, it persists extremely stubbornly in the world of dog-owners and is passed on verbally whenever and wherever people and dogs spend time together. Even puppy-owners who have only had their little dogs living with them for three days and never had a dog or contact with dog-people before believe that they're aware that something like puppy protection exists.

It really is a phenomenon – and indeed a phenomenon that is highly incendiary when Mr Jones's adult dog is not amused when Mrs Smith's impetuous puppy comes bounding up to him to give him a lick on the nose. Screeching puppies that promptly wet themselves and then throw themselves on to their backs are regarded by most humans not as dogs, but as little

angels. By contrast, the adult dog that only really wanted to show the pushy little one how to behave in front of grown-up dogs is soon perceived to be a dog from hell. He is accused of not being normal and in urgent need of a muzzle, because he has not stuck to the rules of puppy protection. While the dog-owners are possibly still arguing over which one of them owns the alleged abnormal dog, both the adult dog and the puppy have undergone experiences entirely of their own.

To a puppy, the whole world is his oyster waiting to be opened and discovered. At every corner there are the most exciting new things to be sniffed at and the wildest discoveries to be made in the form of snails or (really, really great) rubbish bins.

Things always get really jolly when there's another dog in sight, because, after all, he could be a potential playmate that is happy to tumble about boisterously and join in with the wildest games. Only the puppy in our example has not yet found out that not all dogs will behave towards him with extreme consideration and let him carry on. Naturally, this reinforces his conviction that his way of doing it – to race up, head on and tail raised, to every unknown dog – must be absolutely the right one. However, now he

encounters Molly, a seven-year-old bitch, who is known in dog circles as The Boss because she is more than proficient in the doggy times-table and all rules of politeness among fellow canines (she could write the rules of etiquette for dogs) and, apart from this, will not avoid a dispute if, in her opinion, another quadruped fails to show enough respect. So now, the little cuddle-puppy is let loose on this puffed-up female dog. Molly sees that another dog is coming straight towards her and wanting to lick her nose. A faux pas on the part of the puppy and hence a first lesson: never run head-on towards another dog with a raised tail, or there'll be trouble.

Indeed! Molly initially announces what can be expected next with a wrinkled nose and a deep rumbling sound. Then when the puppy does not stop, because his stunt has always worked before, Molly takes stricter measures and rebukes him in a loud voice from above. The puppy's survival instinct kicks in at precisely this moment, he yelps in the highest pitched tones and throws himself on to his back to reveal his exposed little belly and thereby make it clear that he has understood and for his part has absolutely no intention to start a confrontation. From Molly's point of view, the matter is settled and

Whose Sofa is it anyway?

another fellow canine has been taught a significant component of typical canine social behaviour.

Some puppies will need this lesson a whole two, sometimes three, times in a row as they try and stretch it to see whether it really was meant seriously this time, while more sensitive puppies, at least for now, will make a mental note that they ought to approach other dogs with a little more caution. This experience is extremely important for canine infants. They need to learn that they are not allowed to run up to other dogs at all times and in all places in order to greet them.

If they do not learn this, there may be a violent dispute with an unknown dog one day. Nasty injuries can be the result, because the dog that never learned social behaviour will one day get to the age when he defends himself with equal force. In other words, the dog's common interpretation of puppy protection is that nothing can possibly ever happen to a poor innocent mite and every other dog will either ignore him or think he's great.

Therefore, the dog concludes: One needs to be afraid of other dogs and should keep them at a distance by starting to bark and growl even from far away. The main thing is to make sure that they come no closer.

Summary

Puppy protection is a myth that has already led to many injuries in puppies and countless numbers of disputes between people.

Socialisation is important for ensuring that a puppy learns to find his way in the canine world and acquires the manners of typical canine conduct.

This is why, when out with your puppy, you should always put him on the lead first when an unknown dog appears and find out from the other dog-owner whether his dog knows how to deal with puppies. This way, you will avoid excessively close encounters with dogs that could regard the puppy as being a little light snack.

69

There are astonishingly large numbers of people who are able to tell you how they have always been able to let their puppy run free – and that their quadruped never had strife with other dogs. However, never say 'Never'!

Once a negative encounter during puppyhood has been so formative, it can mean repeated difficulties for the rest of the dog's life. It's really not worth the bother, is it?

Mine never does it

Virtually every dog-owner lets these words slip out at least once in his or her quadruped's lifetime. It's awkward, though, that when saying it one forgets that one is dealing with a living creature that has an entirely free will and its own way of looking at things. What's more the saying, 'There's always a first time' can nearly always be tagged on to this statement. There are typical situations where statements such as, 'Mine never does that' need to be hastily revised to, 'Really, he's never done that before.' The following is an overview of the most common situations where both protests can be heard.

Tramp jumps up at a stranger for the first time in his life.

As Mr Jones is strolling in the country-side with his Tramp, who is off the lead as usual, and letting his thoughts wander, Tramp is off somewhere with his head stuck in a mouse hole. Unmoved, Mr Jones continues on his way because there are no problems with Tramp. He won't run up to walkers, won't bother any joggers and he totally ignores strange dogs – as the two-legged half of this relationship, then, Mr Jones hasn't the slightest need to worry and is therefore able to really enjoy his walks.

Mr Jones even rather pities people who have to call their quadruped every time something on two or four legs pops up on the horizon because they'll need to put their dog on the lead. Walks like those must be the opposite of relaxing, he thinks to himself. While he is still abandoned to his thoughts, which are located somewhere between the urgent things that are still on the shopping list and the hope that he may just perhaps have picked the right lottery numbers this time, his Tramp races past him, full of joie de vivre. To wit, he has just had to acknowledge the fact that mouse holes are only a

This one looks as if butter wouldn't melt in his mouth.
But what's going to happen once he's awake?

perfidious plan on the part of small rodents to make his life difficult. There never is a mouse lurking in the hole that he has just dug out.

At this moment, as Mr Jones is thinking with a misty-eyed smile on his face, 'Dogs will be dogs', a blood-curling scream rings out and a woman dressed in light beige is hurling verbal daggers at poor Tramp, who is himself running about her, joyfully wagging his tail and preparing for a verbal counterattack in his turn. Mr Jones immediately notices the many little paw-prints adorning the lady's formerly light-coloured trousers. Now things really get going.

As Mr Jones is being scolded by the lady, he can only stammer bewilderedly, 'Tramp's never done that before though. I don't know why he's done it today...' You can probably guess the rest of the story.

There can be many reasons why a dog that has, for many years, ignored every form of life that he has encountered suddenly discovers his love or displeasure (depending on the situation) for a particular person. Perhaps the biped has moved in an unusual way and startled the dog; perhaps the person is not a dog-lover and showed extreme defensive reactions just at the sight of the quadruped. Whatever it was, this attitude really grabbed the dog's interest. Perhaps his coat blew open in passing, thus appealing to the dog's hunting instinct; perhaps the human even spoke to the dog, therefore giving the impression of wanting to have something to do with him, or maybe he smelled of an unknown dog.

There are many different possibilities, and one can never know which one applied when the incident happened.

Perhaps it is all beyond our understanding and these things simply happen. In any case it is a fact that it can happen, and as a pet-owner you can never be really sure that your own dog will never do something that he has never done before. Animals are unpredictable and it is never possible to forecast their behaviour with one hundred per cent certainty. This is precisely what makes life with them so complicated and yet so wonderful.

So, when unknown people or animals appear, always take care and put the dog on the lead or have the dog lie down so that no tricky situations can develop and the so far stress-free walk can stay that way.

Fido suddenly races
into the woods
during a walk,
remains out of
range for all
recall cues and
stays out of
sight for two
hours before,
worn out but
happy, he
finds his way
back again.

There can be many
reasons why a dog goes
hunting. The explanation
for why a dog suddenly
strays off the path can depend
on many factors.
Perhaps his owner has let him run
much further ahead today than usual.
Perhaps there's usually some fun and
games with the biped in between
times, but today the biped is elsewhere
entirely, lost in his thoughts, or has
brought along his new squeeze or is
on the phone to the office the whole
time. Suddenly Fido has much more
leisure to have a good look at his surroundings and thus discovers things

Even if these border terriers always respected this swan
before, the hunter in them could awaken at any moment.
This is why it is mandatory to put the dog on the lead before
things go wrong.

73

At first glance, this scene is as idyllic as it gets. If dogs venture off on their own here, though, you'll probably need binoculars to find them.

going on in the woods that have previously remained hidden from him. Perhaps a deer has come closer to Fido and owner than ever before, as the two of them are walking through a seldom used part of the woods today and the biped has completely underestimated how strongly the deer path smells and what a big attraction it is for his dog.

There are many reasons here for Fido to go shooting off, and if anybody asks the reply in this case as well, in a tone of conviction, will be: 'He has never done that before, I really don't know what is wrong with him.' If it has happened once, hunting behaviour is never, ever to be taken lightly. To a dog, hunting is self-rewarding behaviour that can only be fought with difficulty. Make a note in advance: if during the course of an excursion there is even a short period when you do not have enough time and leisure to look after your dog, you should at least put him on the lead.

If the horse has already bolted and the quadruped has been out actively on the hunt for something to eat and tear to pieces, it's time to put an end to lead-less excursions through the woods. In this case, as an initial measure the re-call training should be dredged up and performed consistently, and this must be exercised until recall works for cer-tain even when there are lots of distractions. Once it is working again, you can venture into forest regions without a lead once more; if it doesn't work, then professional help absolutely needs to be sought before you start strolling through woods and meadows again, so that the quadruped does not drive all forest inhabitants crazy and potentially fall victim to a huntsman's bullet.

Quite apart from all this, even wild animals have the right to an undisturbed and peaceful life.

The dog that has been a family member for six years bites the three-year-old child out of the blue.

A dog does not bite out of the blue. Dogs are different from humans; they never act out of evil intent or false ambition. Generally, they only snap when provoked. Some dogs snap sooner and more violently, while others have a considerably higher provocation threshold.

I have no idea how often I have already told parents who own a dog that it is totally irresponsible to leave a small child with a dog without supervision. The reply every time was: 'Oh, the dog has never done a thing.' Yet he's been doing something the whole time:

he's been running away from the toddler because the child never would stop grabbing him; he's been baring his teeth because the child was always trying to take away something that was his; he's been growling quietly because someone's been pulling his fur; the list can go on and on.

No one's to blame here: neither the child, who knows no better and wants to explore everything at his or her age, nor the dog, who just needs to be left in peace when he needs his own space and must never be regarded as a living toy. To wit, when the dog has finally had enough and he wants to teach the child some canine manners so that he or she learns to behave differently, his teeth do not sink into thick fur with thick skin, but into delicate child's skin that tears immediately and causes serious pain. Whether the child has just poked the dog's eyes for the umpteenth time because nobody has forbidden it, or whether he or she tried to tear the tasty treat that the dog was about to enjoy on his blanket out of the dog's mouth, in the aftermath nobody's interested in the cause, only in the misfortune that inexplicably came out of the blue. As the saying goes: 'He's never done that before. He was always gentle.'

It is the duty of parents to ensure that both dog and child follow rules, because there is nothing more wonderful for a child than to grow up with a quadruped. Otherwise, avoidable incidents may soon result that, though they generally pass off without serious consequences, still leave behind a bitter aftertaste.

These examples are classics in the field of 'Mine never does that.' Indignant bipeds who claim not to have witnessed their quadrupeds' ambitions to jump up, growl, bite or hunt. The signs are generally always there, but we humans are astonishingly good at ignoring behaviour that we find suspect or would rather not see. But when something that has been threatening to happen does happen, that voice crying out desperately from deep down inside is drowned out by the stammered, 'But really, he's never done that before.' The most interesting thing here is that nearly all dogs that have never done that before go on to do it at least a second or third time, because the biped assumed, after the first time, that it was an oversight and will never ever happen again. Therefore, the behaviour has not been worked on, it has just been ignored, in the hope that this was just a one-off incident.

Ancient wisdoms and our search for a better reality

However, an idea has taken root in the dog's brain – for example: Great! Hunting is fantastic! I can do it as often as I like. And there you have it: a dog that only has one thing on his mind – finding deer tracks in the nearby woods – or that goes off on an active search without waiting for the direct enticement to disappear that he needed the first time around. Every time that he shows this behaviour, it becomes more deeply engrained and is going to be more difficult to get back under control. There is no more hope of a relaxed coexistence with one's dog, à la Lassie; only lots of frown lines, grey hairs and a churning stomach as soon as one steps out of the front door.

These two are getting along well. Nevertheless, child and dog should never be left unsupervised.

Give me five!
Even though bringing up
a dog can be a rocky road,
it will all be fine in the end.

It will all be fine

... as one of my favourite sayings goes. If you have dogs, you should repeat this or a similar encouraging mantra over and over when you are standing alone, yet again, lead in hand, waiting in the rain or cold for the quadruped to return from his foray into the woods.

Chocolates for the neighbour yet again...

Or when you are the unwilling focus of other diners' attention because *Canis familiaris* has put his wondrous voice to use to drive away his alleged adversary, also in the restaurant (who hasn't made a sound, the cowardy-custard). Or when sitting there wrapping yet another apologetic box of chocolates and practising a nice message to say sorry to the neighbour, yet again, for a ploughed-up flowerbed.

Hopefully, at some point one will have internalised one's encouraging mantra to such an extent that one is able to walk, accompanied by a yelping and leaping dog, past the horrified-looking normal person with a downright heroic Zen attitude and entirely without getting caught up in excuses and longing for that fabled hole in the ground to open up. Yes, one day that day will come, and until it does one must work on becoming a little more serene and accepting one's very own botched attempts to bring up the dog or on gradually ironing them out.

This final chapter is intended to be a sort of self-help guide: for one thing, in relation to typical mistakes and how one can iron them out again; and for another, in respect of recognising what is really important when one belongs to that bunch of dog-owners who, from the dog's point of view, behave downright peculiarly from time to time.

Reward, reward, reward

No, not bribery – rewards. Even dogs appreciate the odd motivation boost to keep them in the mood. After all, we humans do not go to work without getting our salaries at the end of the month, and bringing up children doesn't work either without some sort of acknowledgement from mummy and daddy. It's the same thing with our four-legged friends. In the long term, a dog that never receives a reward will lack the motivation to learn new things or do something for his human. However, well-advised rewarding does not mean stuffing one's dog with treats at all times and in all places. He will only get something when he's done something well.

83

How not to become a food dispenser

The important thing is to be inscrutable to the dog and not to debase yourself by becoming a food dispenser. How is this achieved? In terms of theory, it's really easy. If you want to teach the dog something new, reward him for everything that he does that brings him closer to the desired behaviour. Reduce this increased dose of treats by only popping something out of your pocket when the dog shows the intended final behaviour.

Once that is well established, the dog will only receive a reward now and again when he performs the behaviour that the person is looking for.

This way, he will never know when the moment for something tasty is going to come along and will always put his heart into the training. It is the same principle that turns humans into compulsive gamblers: you don't win every time, because that would make the whole thing boring, but every now and then you are up there with the winners and that keeps the interest going. We're also trying to keep the dog in the mood by maintaining his suspense: maybe today he'll hit that jackpot.

Rewards in the form of food or toys can be used as a cunning distraction, depending on what the individual dog likes best. This can be when encountering other quadrupeds that the dog does

Toys are also a good means of motivation.

84

not like, for example. Hold something good in front of his nose to distract him and use this to draw his gaze from the trigger. If he then allows the other dog to walk past and keeps his mouth shut at the same time, we reward him with a treat. The important thing is to distract the dog before he has managed to take a good look at the alleged antagonist; otherwise there will barely be the chance to call him back to the here and now. At first, it also helpful to walk slightly off the path, so that there is a sufficient gap between your dog and the unknown one. Generally speaking, with the aid of concentration and treats, you can relatively soon have a dog that, in anticipation of a reward (which, in the case of this 'problem', he should receive for as long as possible and on regular basis), has the appearance of being virtually a gentle little lamb instead of a dog gone berserk as soon as an unknown dog is sighted.

As a dog-owner, then, you have a choice: dog gone berserk and, after a walk, ears ringing with yapping and a dislocated spine from the dog straining on the lead; o having treats on hand at all times and, in return, a tolerably calm and peaceful quadruped on the end of the lead. You can always decide whether to accept and stick with a mistake, or work on problems actively. Isn't that great?

Why does it have to happen to me, of all people?

A dog that does not obey one hundred per cent in all situations or fails to run up to his human, beaming with joy, the first time he's called is no exception. Time and time again there are situations where the quadruped fails to perform a cue as reliably as he has done a thousand times before. Days where something happens for the first time and the dog-owner returns home dejectedly and asks himself what he's actually been training for all these months or years, and why he has this dog at all, and tells himself that he could have done everything differently if he'd tried to get his quadruped to obey as nicely or behave as decently as the dog who joins them for walkies.

Every now and then, some bipeds even get so fed up that they sink into a kind of depressive state when they go walking with their dog because they never stop asking themselves questions: Why won't he obey? Why does he always pull on the lead? What have I done to deserve it? Virtually everybody who owns a dog will at some point happen upon the question:

No two dogs are alike. Even dogs choose who they want to talk to. (Photo: Weires)

'Why my dog, and why is it happening to me of all people?'

This may be the immediate reaction of any biped driven mad by a dog when another exorbitant cleaning bill flutters through the letterbox because the darling had to greet someone with muddy paws again. Maybe this reaction doesn't come until the phenomenon of neighbours with dogs suddenly changing direction to avoid 'that person' with the yelping and leaping dog gone berserk becomes a noticeably frequent one. Perhaps this question pops up when you find yourself back in the orthopaedic waiting room because Fido has dislocated your shoulder by yanking on the lead again.

Never give up!

Training a dog is a process that continues throughout his life and in some cases, in certain respects, it is going to come to nothing. At some point, we have to concede that anything that fails despite repeated training is some kind of personality trait.

If your dog fails to master something no matter how hard you try, regardless of how often you tinker about with it, you should come to accept it as an individual factor in the quadruped's personality (though only as long as it is not dangerous either for humans or animals or the dog himself!).

So he always stretches out on mother-in-law's favourite armchair. So what? Perhaps she, too, has idiosyncrasies that the people around her have to accept. In the quadruped's case, though, one should still bring along a blanket to protect the armchair.

A tip from me:

Do not leap onto the defensive when people point out minor training shortcomings. This is because, with time, precisely this defensive reaction is going to draw everybody's attention only to these mistakes that we've committed at some point during the upbringing and not to all the other wonderful personality traits that make us love our own dog with such blind adoration. Other dogs make their mistakes, too. No dog is perfect. They are animals and should be allowed to behave as such, at least as far as possible. It's only to be expected that not everything is going to work impeccably and at all times; after all, this is something that we humans can't even achieve with machines.

Ignoring stupid remarks

Try to ignore negative comments from other dog-owners and always go over and over the reasons in your mind why your own dog, as far as you personally are concerned, is the best quadruped in the world.

Yes, there are dogs with which things seem to be working beautifully when you see them: dogs that do not pull on the lead, that won't flex their muscles when other dogs wander into their path, that lie obediently next to their human in the café and doze. Yet many of these quadrupeds also have dark secrets that give their owners grey hairs and that never reveal themselves when the average dog-owner is close by, and some of these dogs are quite simply one thing:

Boring!

Picture this: you get up in the morning and are greeted by your dog courteously, but not too effusively; later, you pick up the lead and leave the house with a dog that can barely be felt. The whole walk through, you don't even notice that you've got a dog with you because he never runs away too far and only greets other dogs briefly (but then returns to following you like a shadow). He's not even visible at home, as he lies politely in his basket and waits for you to tell him what to do next. A vision of horror! After all, one of the exciting things in a dog-owner's life is that you never know what is going to happen next.

As a human-and-dog team, you need to form a bond and experience the highs and lows together. After a certain time you will then know exactly how the dog is going to react in different situations. This is the way life goes: we are all individuals.

So, calling a dog with minor failings in manners (or simply unique personality traits) your own is the greatest thing in the world, after all, and nothing to be ashamed of, no matter what other dog-owners or dogless people say. Therefore, a little bit of ignoring when it comes to critics makes life much, much easier and, above all, considerably more relaxed and enjoyable.

Therefore, in the event that somebody launches tirades of curses because the beloved quadruped is stomping, muddy-pawed but as happy as can be and with head held high, through the shopping centre again, pulling his biped from one window display to the next whilst yapping away to tell the whole world that he's around, then do

It's allowed for one's own dog to be the greatest, the most wonderful and most beautiful dog in the world! When we're aware of what we love him for, we can easily turn a blind eye to minor shortcomings.
(Photo: Slawik)

Looking beautiful and being ultra-obedient too: you can't have it all, eh?

as your dog does. Straighten your back and puff out your chest; grin into everybody's face when they stare at you and your 'damn dog' and show the world that you belong to the happiest and most relaxed group of people in our society: namely, to the group with the best cholesterol and blood-pressure levels – dog-owners.

You must not spoil the proven positive aspects – the many walks in the countryside and the relaxing and blood-pressure-lowering process of running one's fingers through the dog's fur – by taking all those sidelong glances or indignant accusations too much to heart. If you did, this would immediately cancel out all these good points and all that remained would be our love for our dog, who always loves us bipeds the way we are without asking why or wanting to change us. We should give him exactly the same love in return because, after all, it is we who are trying to mould the animal to our society and its rules. We want to change him so that he complies with our way of viewing things – and in return, we can at least accept that the things that our dog's unique character offers us are not always perfect.

I am a star in his world

Admiration, devoted respect, unshakeable loyalty and disinterested love. These are the emotions that true fans hold for their stars.

Practically everybody who observes this euphoria, this enthusiasm in the media wishes, somewhere deep down inside, to be loved and revered in just the same way one day. The thing that almost everybody forgets, or only realises dimly, is that, as a dog-owner, you have a real fan, a living creature who loves you unconditionally, follows you everywhere and – without asking why – would walk through fire for you, his human. There is a very good reason why the dog is known as man's best friend.

A dog regards his human from a very specific viewpoint. Let me have a go at describing a dog's daily routine and the way a dog views his day:

My human wakes up and joins me out of doors. This is just wonderful, because I can't sneak out by myself – he makes sure that I can enjoy some movement, can scan and write over my rivals' scents. He guides me and defines the best route. I am not alone, he is there for me.

Now we are back at our camp and he gives me something to eat. He must be a hero, because every day, without apparent effort, there's always fresh food for me. Only a truly great hunter can get hold of so much food that there's enough for everybody. This is why I admire him.

Now he is going and leaving me on my own. It's hard for me to wait for him to come back, but so far he's never disappointed me and has always returned. I wonder whether that will be the case today as well?

Oh, I really, really hope so, because without him I cannot exist.

Yes, I can hear him coming down the path. In a moment he'll open the door and come in. I just cannot wait to say hello to him. It's so wonderful to see him again and do something together again. I wonder whether we'll go on another hunting expedition together?

It doesn't matter, the main thing is that he's back. I knew that he would not let me down. Yes, we're going off on another tour of discovery together, and he's always thinking up new things on these trips. Is there anything better than my human?

No, there just can't be.

Yes

Every dog is unique –
let's love him the way he is!
(Photo: Röder)

Our dogs are our dependants, and they know it. They show us love and absolute trust, and we should show them the same thing in return. Like every star, we have our shortcomings, sides to us that are not perfect, but to our fan – our dog – that doesn't matter. He doesn't realise that we often behave selfishly when we would rather stay cosy and warm indoors than take a walk with our dog. He doesn't apologise to other dogs when we bring him into yet another embarrassing situation because our verbal means of expression was in stark contrast with our body language. He accepts us the way we are, and we acknowledge this by slandering his character in front of other people? Why not simply model ourselves on our dog and respect him the way he is?

   Looking at the behaviours that bother us in our own dogs, we are going to have be honest and admit that we are not entirely innocent in the case. Jumping up, because the dog has not had enough training in not

A proper little character. There's even lots to learn if we accept that our dog has his own personality.

doing it; running away, because one has set the wrong examples or hasn't practised recall enough; yelping at other dogs because, instead of training, one has preferred the simple solution of a detour or retreat. In many cases the blame falls on human convenience, which has left the dog no other choice than to develop certain ways of behaving. Let's stick to our obligations. Let's occasionally play the role of the star, a little aloof from the here and now in his own little world, his own reality, and wise not to let that criticism even register. This way, life with a dog in our society is going to be much, much better.

However often we should attempt to ignore disgruntled people and their constant complaints about us and our four-legged friends, we are the dog-owners and as such should try and aim for peaceful cohabitation in our society.

Dogs have featured in more and more negative headlines in recent years, and many people feel justified in their fear or disinclination towards our beloved quadrupeds.

WOW! Man, I think you're great.

If you follow the canine rules of etiquette,
you can take dogs almost anywhere,
even the golf course.
(Photo: Widmann)

Etiquette
hints
for dog-owners

Unfortunately there are dog-owners who aren't great publicity for the broader group of dog-people and who hence make all our lives unnecessary difficult. By following one or two rules for living with dogless people, one can make this world a tiny bit better, a world with more understanding for dogs. In the following, I provide an overview of the most important etiquette hints for dog-owners, which, if followed, can help to avoid trouble and misunderstandings:

Etiquette hint no. 1:

Scoop poop.

Even for dog-lovers, stepping into quadrupeds' doings is something that may cause retching. How bad it must be for ordinary fellow citizens who may not be too fond of the animals in the first place!

Especially if it just can't be avoided and the dog does his business alongside or even on the path, it should be a matter of course to take corresponding measures. Yes, there are lovelier things to do – but in this case, one must never shirk one's own responsibilities.

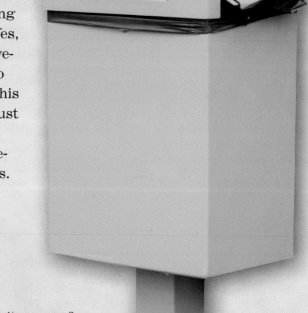

Etiquette hint no. 2:

Always put the dog on the lead when walkers, joggers or cyclists come your way.

As much as we would like it sometimes, parks, woods or paths alongside fields do not belong to us dog-owners. We share them with all kinds of other people who do not wish to be pestered by our quadrupeds, so even when we have somehow managed to teach our dog not to greet other people, we should put him on the lead. For lots of different reasons, many people are scared of dogs and do not feel particularly comfortable about having a big dog approach them.

This situation is definitely not the best one in which to let dog-owner aloofness prevail. Lead on, walk past, friendly hello – this should be the procedure here.

You should always have a little bag for poop removal in your pocket when out with your dog.
Special dog-poop bins are now provided in parks and very busy places.
(Photo: Widmann)

This big Landseer is still dry, but the chance that he's about to jump enthusiastically into the water and then shake himself out thoroughly is big. Anybody standing close by would get soaking wet.
(Photo: Kuhn)

Etiquette hint no. 3:

Do not let the wet dog shake himself dry next to strangers.

During the hot season, it is laudable to give the quadruped the opportunity to splash about in cool water to his heart's content. Generally, however, in weather like this there also tend to be other humans nearby who want to enjoy the weather and their free time in peace. So when a soaking-wet dog shakes himself right close by them, spraying a mixture of dirt, hairs and water to all four corners of the earth in the process, understandably the prospect of an all-out fight is no longer quite so distant. Not every person on this earth is charmed by having their white linen trousers adorned with dirty blotches, and not all people who spend time close to the water walk around in dirtproof, waterproof, walkies-friendly clothing. This is why you should show consideration for the neatly dressed people – who generally wish to remain so – and call the dog straight back to you as soon as he gets out of the water so that he only refreshes his own people with a cool shower.

Etiquette hint no. 4:

Never feed strange dogs without asking their owners for permission.

This is a topic that doesn't seem to want to go away at dog schools and seminars. All the other dogs are so pretty and look so sweet that one just has to slip them a treat when one's own dog gets one or otherwise they'll be sad. Resist the impulse and save the treat for your own dog.

Never mind that fights may break out even if you only feed your own dog while five others are sitting next to you, drooling away; you may well get (quite rightly, in my opinion) a harsh verbal slap in the face from another dog-owner if he notices you feeding his dog. Not a few people spend quite a lot of their quadrupeds' lives convincing them that it is never worth begging from strangers, no matter how nice these strangers may look.

However, dogs that spend a lot of time at various dog schools often find out that one only needs to look interested enough to get to enjoy forbidden sweeties, too. On the next stroll through the town, the dog may even

Preferably not, even with your own dog.
Otherwise, there is the risk that he'll enquire
after leftovers with other diners in the beer
garden.

Etiquette hint no. 5:

Never let your own free-running quadruped run to a dog that's on the lead without being asked.

If you come across a dog that's on the lead while your own is running free, call your dog back to you. Of course, this can only work if your dog has learned to react as soon as he is called. You then put him on the lead and either walk briskly past the other dog or discuss (at a distance) with the unknown dog-owner whether you would like to let both dogs run free. Please do not expect to be overwhelmed with friendly words if your quadruped runs up to the dog on the lead without being asked. Besides annoyance and insecurity, this may cause the other dog-owner to feel that you're indifferent to what's happening.

The other person will presumably have his or her own reasons for leaving the dog on the lead. Maybe the other dog is injured and is therefore not allowed to run, and now your quadruped is causing a scar to reopen. Or, you spend days afterwards watching your dog closely because he may have

beg from everybody or bark at anyone holding something edible. Again, the only thing that's left is a stammered, 'He never does that usually, honest,' before a hasty retreat is beaten.

Either both dogs run free or both are on the lead.
The situation can always be awkward if only
one dog is on the lead.
(Photo: Kuhn)

caught something from the other one. Maybe the dog on the lead is a bitch on heat, whose scent is still making your male dog's blood rage even after you've hauled him off her back and towed him off hundreds of metres away in the opposite direction. Maybe the other dog, though, for a variety of different reasons, is incompatible with other quadrupeds. Your bewildered, stammered words: 'But they normally sort it out between themselves without major injuries,' as you search for your address and telephone number for the purpose of the imminent vet's bill, do not make the guilty feelings any smaller.

There can be a thousand and one reasons for not allowing a dog to run off the lead. Show respect for this, because you, too, could soon be having to walk your dog on the lead and noting with horror how unpleasant it can be when totally unknown quadrupeds come racing up to you.

A few words in closing

Laughter is always closely followed by tears, both in everyday life and when bringing up a dog.

As soon as you bring a quadruped home, he is a member of your family, with all his peculiarities, whether you like it or not. You are suddenly confronted with questions that never occurred to you before, or at least only briefly. How do I bring him up properly? How do I keep him busy? Where can I get good food? Will the hotel put us up even if we've got a dog with us? How can I best explain to my boss that I'm going to be late yet again because the vet has called us back?

Question upon question, many of which can be answered quickly but others, by contrast, take up a lot of room in our thoughts and in our everyday lives. Why did he nip at the other dog? What was his reason for just running right across the road and nearly getting run over? How can I teach him that the postman is not a burglar? Why is the neighbourhood conspiring against us? It is not always easy to live with a dog. You get sidelong glances when the dog is barking, when he's dirty, when he does his business or even when you are just being boisterous and having fun and games with him. So many times, the quadruped drives us to the brink of insanity because we have instilled so many bad habits into him that we feel we need to justify ourselves to the whole world.

Yet, for all the things that annoy us in all matters canine, one thing is for certain, once we've listened earnestly to

that voice deep down inside: we would never let him down. We wouldn't be able to live without the love that he shows us every day. We would miss the tears that we have laughed with many a time because he acted so oddly during our games.

We dog-owners have hit the jackpot: we have a living creature at our side who loves us with all our defects, who accepts all our weaknesses and always takes us as we are.

Our dog has learned to cope with living in a world that doesn't take all that much trouble to learn his language: a world in which he is required to learn, within a short space of time, a totally alien verbal language and an ambiguous body language, and he always does his best to interpret correctly what

we're asking him to do. Let's help him by trying to make it easy for him, with clear words and the attempt to read his thoughts, at least once in a while. Then, while things may not resolve themselves from one day to the next, and there will definitely be no boring, perfect dogs all around us, perhaps we'll stop having quite so many problems.

The best thing about our four-legged friend is his individual character. This is what makes him so wonderfully unique. Let's just live with the small defects that he has and that, in so many cases, we have instilled into him. The wonderful life with our dog is much too short to cry over minor shortcomings to such an extent that it puts a cloud over our relationship with him.

And always remember: humour is laughing in spite of it all.

Thank You

Of course, there is a whole range of people every author wishes to thank at some point in the book. To avoid being too long-winded, in my case I will restrict myself to the narrowest core of those to whom I want to express a giant MERCI with all my heart.

First place, of course, is occupied by my three dogs (who would, admittedly, certainly be happier with a bone than with a written mark of favour). They were and are my greatest teachers and without the totally different characters of Laska, Pearl and Cloud and the repeatedly renewed challenges they place before me, I would never have got as far as I have done as concerns my understanding of bringing up dogs and cohabitation with quadrupeds – and the story is far from over. I hope that I immortalised my darlings in this way somehow – they have honestly deserved it. Girls, I love you the way you are. Thank you for the joy you bring me every single day and for the deep trust you place in me. I hope that I live up to it.

Naturally, the most important person in my life will not be allowed to escape unscathed either. It is a very special thing to find a partner who shares this passion for animals. Without my darling Ralph I would never have finished writing this book. Many thanks for your constant support and for your unfaltering belief in me. I know that I can be very demanding (almost as demanding as dogs are sometimes) – we love you!

A very special thank you goes to Dorothee Dahl from Cadmos Verlag – nobody writing a first draft could wish for a better proofreader. THANK YOU for everything.

And to whom is this book dedicated? Naturally, to all more or less desperate dog parents who are now perhaps able to summon up a new, alternative understanding for their quadrupeds and are taking much of it with more humour.

It is also a matter of concern to me to refer to two very special people: Bea Urban, who steps in with tireless dedication for border collies and many other dogs that are unwanted. Many thanks Bea for everything you have already achieved for so many animals and will be achieving in the future. Without you I would never have found my Pearl and I say a mental word of thanks to you every day for this wonderful dog. You are one of the most remarkable people it has ever been my honour to meet. For everyone wanting to find out more about her work: www.bordercollie-rescue.org.

The next person who, for me, gloriously exemplifies self-sacrifice and canine knowledge is Gesa Kuhn from www.countrydog.de. Through Gesa I have learned a crazy amount about border collies and discovered an entirely new laid-back attitude towards dealing with my dogs. Gesa, you are a wonderful person and it is fascinating, again and again, to watch and experience you dealing with dogs. You are like an angel in the canine world.

CADMOS

DOG - GUIDES

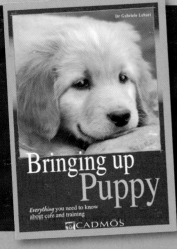

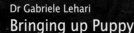

Dr Gabriele Lehari
Bringing up Puppy

In this accessible guide, you will find a wealth of information about puppies and puppyhood, how to care for and train them, helping to ensure that they enjoy this precious time, and that your puppy develops into a reliable partner.

96pp, Paperback, £9.95
ISBN 978-386127-959-4

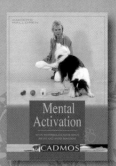

Uli Köppel	**Christina Sondermann**	**Manuela Zaitz**	**Anders Hallgren**
## The Pack Concept	## Playtime for your Dog	## Trick School for Dogs	## Mental Activation

This book presents some amazing new truths about dealing and communicating with dogs, based on behavioural biology. Uli Köppel, a pupil of kynologist Eberhard Trumler, focuses on relationship training for the human-dog team, in place of exploitative training, to help us understand the special relationship between humans and dogs.

128pp, Paperback, £14.95
ISBN 978-386127-958-7

Games play an important role in the development and well-being of dogs. This book will help discover and employ games and activities on an everyday basis, using everyday objects, that both owners and dogs will enjoy, and that will contribute towards a dog's fitness and training.

128pp, Hardbound, £19.95
with jacket
ISBN 978-386127-92

Everybody can give a dog a good mental or physical work-out at home or during a daily walk with the use of dog tricks. This book presents fun and challenging tricks to keep a dog eager and interested. Numerous photos make the practical application of tasks and exercises simple and encourage readers to 'try this at home'.

ISBN 978-386127-960-0

Dogs need to encounter and overcome physical and mental challenges to remain stimulated, happy and well. Anders Hallgren describes many simple exercises designed to engage and improve a dog's senses. 'A wealth of fun ideas for increasing the interaction between you and your dog.' – Your Dog

96pp, Paperback, £12.95
ISBN 978-386127-927-3

www.cadmos.co.uk   CADMOS